HEAVEN

WHAT A WONDERFUL PLACE!

Kenny Boles

 COLLEGE PRESS
PUBLISHING COMPANY
Joplin, Missouri

International Standard Book Number 0-89900-830-5

CONTENTS

STUDIES FOR SMALL GROUPS

Welcome to the *Studies for Small Groups* series from College Press. This series is designed for simplicity of use while giving insight into important issues of the Christian life. Some, like the present volume, will be topical studies. Others will examine a passage of Scripture for the day-to-day lessons we can learn from it.

A number of possible uses could be made of this study. Because there are a limited number of lessons, the format is ideal for new or potential Christians who can begin the study without feeling that they are tied into an overly long commitment. It could also be used for one or two months of weekly studies by a home Bible study group. The series is suitable for individual as well as group study.

Of course, any study is only as good as the effort you put into it. The group leader should study each lesson carefully before the group study session, and if possible, come up with additional Scriptures and other supporting material. Although study questions are provided for each lesson, it would also be helpful if the leader can add his or her own questions.

Neither is it necessary to complete a full lesson in one class period. If the discussion is going well, don't feel that you have to cut it off to fit time constraints, as long as the discussion is related to the topic and not off on side issues.

Because more people believe in heaven than believe in hell, because most people say they want (even expect) to go there, but there are so many contradictory ideas of what heaven will be like, College Press is happy to present this new 8-lesson study in the *Studies for Small Groups* series, *Heaven: What a Wonderful Place!*

HEAVEN: WHAT A WONDERFUL PLACE!

Have you thought much about heaven lately? (What will it look like? Who will be there? What will you do with all that time on your hands? Could you ever get tired of a *really long* praise service?)

Maybe it's wrong to speculate. After all, none of us has been there yet. And people who teach wild ideas about heaven usually end up starting weird cults, don't they? Maybe we should just conclude that all the Scriptures are only figurative, and no one knows anything about our eternal home. Whatever it turns out to be, we can just resign ourselves to our fate.

But maybe it's worse not to speculate. In our fear of teaching an incorrect picture of heaven, sometimes we wind up teaching no picture at all. Heaven becomes an empty address for a distant "someday," and we show little eagerness to get there. Our friends must think it curious that we claim to have won a one-way ticket to some tropical Paradise, but we rarely talk about what it will be like when we get there! So let's do a study on heaven.

We need to have two ground rules. First, all our ideas must grow out of what God has revealed to us in his Word. No ideas can be valid if they contradict what God has explicitly said. Second, as long as we remember that our ideas are only tentative, there is plenty of room for a bit of "sanctified imagination." This is especially true when our ideas can be shown to be the natural, logical end toward which Scripture is pointing. Sharing our ideas and dreams about heaven can be inspirational, informative, and fun!

One thing we know for sure: heaven will be good. Really good. Every piece of evidence we can dig from the Bible confirms it. Our gracious God and our loving Savior have gone to great lengths to prepare us a place, and to be sure we get there. When we finally are promoted to our Father's house, we will probably blink, grin, and shout, "Good heaven! What a wonderful place!"

1

ONE

DOES HEAVEN EXIST?

In some circles, heaven seems to have fallen on hard times. America's favorite atheist, Madalyn Murray O'Hair, says heaven is "a delusional dream of the unsophisticated minds of the ill-educated clergy." Former Harvard professor Alfred North Whitehead asks, "Can you imagine anything more appallingly idiotic than the Christian idea of heaven?" The whole scene of eternal bliss appears simply too good to be true. Is it just wishful thinking to hope for "pie in the sky by-and-by"?

Many churches seem to think that the idea of heaven is old-fashioned. Martin Marty, a religious historian at the University of Chicago, recalls hearing many sermons on heaven and hell in his childhood, but says, "Now the only time you hear of heaven is when somebody has died." David Wells, a professor at more conservative Gordon-Conwell Theological Seminary, notes, "We would expect to hear of it in the Evangelical churches, but I don't hear it at all." It does seem like we used to sing more often, "Just a few more weary days and then I'll fly away." Perhaps modern life at the turn of the millennium is just not as weary as it used to be! Perhaps when life is good, heaven is less necessary.

Still, in spite of it all, most people say they believe in heaven. A poll taken by TIME/CNN in 1997 asked, "Do you believe in the existence of heaven, where people live forever with God after they die?" A strong majority of 81% said, "Yes." The hope of heaven seems deeply woven into the fabric of the American soul. It may surface only in times of emergency, but the underlying belief in heaven is still there. Why do so many people still believe in heaven? Is it right and reasonable? Let's see what we can learn.

WHAT CAN WE LEARN FROM NATURE?

Every autumn we watch the grass die, the flowers disappear, and the trees go bare. All of nature seems to be dying around us. Winter sets in, and life grows bleak and cold. Then, just when we think we can stand it no longer, signs of life return. Sprigs of green grass and flowers push up from the ground; trees bud; birds sing. In the cycle of nature, death is followed by life. Perhaps this lesson in nature is the reason all tribes of men in every continent have historically developed some kind of belief in life after death.

The Bible confirms this natural lesson. Jesus explained his own resurrection by the imagery of the kernel of wheat which falls to the earth, dies, and is reborn to even greater life (John 12:24). Just as the created world teaches basic facts about God (Rom 1:20), so it provides a beautiful picture of death followed by life. *Nature prepares us to accept the reality of heaven.*

WHAT CAN WE LEARN FROM HUMAN NATURE?

Nature prepares us to accept the reality of heaven.

As we grow through each phase of our lives, something wonderful happens to most of us. We begin life knowing nothing; by adulthood we know an astonishing number of things. We begin without the ability to speak or walk or reason; by adulthood we have honed these skills into productive lives. Defiant teenage

> If heaven is real, then climbing upward through life makes sense.

rebels become mature, responsible adults. Even in our fallenness, we are making progress — in at least some areas of life.

But what is the purpose of this progress, this maturing? Is the goal of life the rest home and the grave? What is the good of learning, improving, and developing into a better person? It would appear that just when we finally achieve that goal, it is too late to do us any good. The "survival of the fittest" cannot explain our drive to become mature, for it is at the point of final maturity that we fail to survive. There must be something of lasting value in the maturing of human nature, or life is simply not worthwhile.

A person lives a good life when that life is spent aspiring, learning, and maturing. The good life is obviously the life that is spent preparing for the next. *If heaven is real, then climbing upward through life makes sense* (See Phil 3:12-14). If heaven is real, then maturing has a logical purpose. Therefore, what we can observe in the best of human nature tells us there ought to be a heaven.

WHAT CAN WE LEARN FROM GOD'S NATURE?

The nature of God makes the idea of heaven both reasonable and necessary. God, for instance, is completely just and fair. But our world is full of injustice and inequity. Babies with horrible birth defects will never run and play; children in famine-stricken lands will not survive beyond childhood. Sickness, pain, and death fill the earth. A God of justice requires a place and a time where all this can be set right. When the world is once again the way God wants it to be, there will be "no more death or mourning or crying or pain" (Rev 21:4).

God, moreover, is a God of an everlasting love. He desired to have intimate fellowship with Adam and Eve; he desires to have the same with us. He has not loved us only to throw us away. The goal of his love — the requirement of his own divine nature — is eternal fellowship with us. This can only be fulfilled when we go to live forever in our Father's house. *The nature of God demands that there be such a place called heaven.*

BUT HAS ANYBODY BEEN THERE?

So far we have established that it is reasonable and right that people should believe that heaven exists. Nature, human nature, and God's nature all seem to require that there be such a place. But this is all rather philosophical. So let's cut to the chase: Has anyone ever seen it? Has anybody been there? Is there firsthand testimony that heaven exists?

First, we should examine the evidence of Moses and Elijah. On a mountaintop in Galilee they stood beside Jesus, conversing with him about his upcoming departure from this life (Luke 9:30-31). At this point in history Moses had been dead for at least 1300 years and Elijah had been gone for nearly 900 years. Yet here they were, alive and well. How could this be? It was because God had safely protected his servant Moses, and had triumphantly carried Elijah to heaven in a whirlwind. One of the disciples who saw Moses and Elijah with the transfigured Jesus that day was Simon Peter. He later wrote, "We did not follow cleverly invented sto-

The nature of God demands that there be such a place called heaven.

12

ries . . . we were eyewitnesses of his majesty. . . . we were with him on the sacred mountain" (2 Pet 1:16-18).

Has anyone been to this place called heaven? Many have!

We should also consider the evidence of the apostle Paul. Probably speaking of himself in 2 Corinthians 12:1-4, he tells of a man who was "caught up to the third heaven." (In the language of the day, the first heaven was the atmosphere we breathe, the second heaven was the sky and stars above, while the third heaven was the dwelling of God.) This man was "caught up to paradise" (v. 4) where he heard inexpressible things that man is not permitted to tell.

Has anyone been to this place called heaven? Many have! God is not the God of dead men in tombs; he is the God of living men in heaven. He is (not "was") the God of Abraham, Isaac, and Jacob (Matt 22:31-32). He is the One whom Stephen sees, with Jesus standing to his right, as the martyr is welcomed into heaven (Acts 7:56). He is the one around whom the saints throng in the revelation seen by John (Rev 7:9-12).

The best and final answer to the question, "Has anyone been there?" is Jesus himself. He repeatedly called himself "the one who has come down from above." He did the things he had seen the Father doing, and spoke the things the Father told him to speak. We cannot believe in Jesus without believing in heaven! To his worried followers in the upper room, Jesus said knowingly, "In my Father's house are many rooms . . . . I am going there to prepare a place for you" (John 14:2). On the cross the next day Jesus said to a penitent thief, "I tell you the truth, today you will be with me in paradise" (Luke 23:43).

In effect, Jesus has made the same promise to all of us. He said he would return to the Father, and then he would come back for us (John 14:3). Presently he sits at the right hand of God, but ultimately he is coming again. Then all God's children will be gathered into his glorious presence. (See 1 Thess 4:13-18.)

DOES IT MATTER TO ME RIGHT NOW?

Even if heaven is real, we must admit that it still seems a long way off. So what difference does it make to my life right now? First, the reality of heaven gives meaning to life. It helps us understand the big picture. In the face of injustice and inequity, in times of suffering, at the hour of death our hope of heaven brings life into sharper focus. Similarly, in times of prosperity and in moments of pleasure, the reality of future bliss gives us perspective. If we can start looking at every daily event from the vantage point of eternity, we will gain great insight into the deep truths of life.

Second, *a lively hope of heaven helps us give things their proper priority.* When our eyes are fixed on heaven, we won't sweat the little stuff. Who cares if our bodies are falling apart — we're going to get new ones! Who cares if one political party gets ahead of the other one — our real citizenship is in heaven! This does not mean that we should take a reckless and irresponsible attitude toward life, but it does mean that we recognize which things are temporary and which things are eternal. By the way, when churches have their eyes fixed on heaven, they don't worry much about why the high school classroom was painted purple. Folks who are excited about going to heaven rarely stop and fuss with fellow pilgrims.

Third, the hope of heaven motivates us to persevere. Permit me a simple analogy. Each year I spend a few weeks in church camp. Sometimes the weather is miserable, the food is

> A lively hope of heaven helps us give things their proper priority.

14

bad, the campers are rude, and the bunk bed is impossible! When this is my predicament, I put a smile on my face and think to myself, "Friday is coming. My troubles will soon be over. I'll get in my car, turn on the air conditioner, and head for home. Friday's coming — I'm going home!" With heaven just around the corner, our present troubles seem much smaller. With an eternal reward in view, even martyrdom can be accepted. Heaven gives us reason to persevere.

> Heaven is not only a reasonable idea, it is a necessary truth.

Heaven is real. When each of us faces our own death, there will still be life for us in heaven. When the earth as we know it has been destroyed, there will still be heaven. Skeptics may shout against it, but God's word stands true: we are receiving a kingdom that cannot be shaken (Heb 12:28). *Heaven is not only a reasonable idea, it is a necessary truth.* It is the key that unlocks the understanding of life, puts things in their proper priority, and gives us strength to persevere. Heaven is real — and it is good!

REFLECTING ON LESSON ONE

1. Why do some intelligent people say there is no heaven?

2. What is there in life that points to greater life after death?

3. How does the nature of God require the kind of heaven the Bible describes?

4. What if Jesus had said to the penitent thief, "I think it might just be possible that someday you and I may be in a better place"? What specific differences are found in Luke 23:43? How do these differences matter?

5. Would you say that churches are talking less about heaven? If we are talking less about heaven, what other topics have replaced it?

6. What would you do differently if you knew there were no life after death?

7. What difference does the hope of heaven make in your life right now?

2
T W O

WHO WILL BE THERE?

All right. We've established that heaven is real — philosophically and scripturally real. Now it's time to let it become real — personally real — for you. Imagine you have just gone to heaven. What do you see? Anything? Nothing? Let's start filling in that vague, empty picture. We will begin by inserting the inhabitants of heaven.

ANGELS, ANGELS, ANGELS

The Bible's pictures of heaven nearly always include a host of angels. When we get to heaven we will see the seraphs (the Hebrew plural is seraphim). These are the six-winged creatures who fly around the throne of God crying, "Holy! Holy! Holy!" (Isa 6:2 and Rev 4:8). What intensity there is in the purity of their worship! Along with the seraphs we will see the cherubs (the Hebrew plural is cherubim). These creatures look like winged lions with human faces. God is "enthroned between the cherubim," symbolically in the tabernacle and eternally in heaven (Ps 99:1). After the fall God posted cherubs at the Garden of Eden to prevent Adam and Eve from returning. But in heaven we will have nothing to fear from seraphs, or cherubs, or any other kind of angel. *The angels exist to care for our needs* (Heb 1:14). In fact, we who are children of God will have the authority of judgment over the angels (1 Cor 6:3). Significantly, it was for us — not for angels — that Jesus brought salvation (Heb 2:16).

In heaven we will see the great archangel Michael. He led the forces of God in the great war against Satan — and won! (See Rev 12:7.) Just think how interesting it will be to hear all about that! I also plan to ask him about that business with the "prince of Persia" in Daniel 10:13. Have God's angels been fighting for us behind the scenes all along?

The angel we know the most about is Gabriel, God's special messenger. He is the one who spoke to Daniel, explaining God's vision (Dan 8:16; 9:21). More famously, it was Gabriel who told Zechariah about the birth of John the Baptist and told Mary about the birth of Jesus (Luke 1:19,26). The unnamed angel who spoke later to Joseph was probably also Gabriel (Matt 1:20). Do you suppose we will get to meet this mighty angel? What a story he could tell about the look on Mary's face when he said, "Good news! God likes you, and so you're going to be pregnant!" With all these angels around, heaven certainly won't be boring!

PEOPLE, PEOPLE, PEOPLE

There are going to be a lot of people in heaven. When they gather around the throne of God, they will form an innumerable multitude from every nation, tribe, people, and language. When God is honored, he deserves to have more than just a few people show up!

> **The angels exist to care for our needs.**

18

Who will all these people be? Some of them will be people we have been ignoring — the homeless, the beggars, the losers of life. God seems especially eager to get folks like the beggar Lazarus up to heaven. Do you suppose we will feel embarrassed for all the times we passed

> The great throng of heaven will include people from a lot of different churches.

them by? And some of the people of heaven will be people of color. Any color. Every color. God made them all and will gladly welcome them into his neighborhood. If God has a sense of humor, he might have some really interesting seating arrangements at the wedding feast of the Lamb! And some of the people in heaven will be people we just don't like. Do you suppose that God has forgiven certain people and you still haven't? It sometimes bothers me to think that God can embrace former murderers, rapists, etc. There will be sinners in heaven! What on earth can God see in such people? I don't want to make heaven seem unattractive, but we really should face up to the fact that God's whole family will be there.

The great throng of heaven will include people from a lot of different churches. Since no denomination has an exclusive franchise on total truth, God is going to have to forgive all of us for our areas of partial misunderstanding. Like a wise shepherd, the Lord knows those who belong to him and will gather them from every corner of the religious world. In heaven we will find out which of our petty arguments were irrelevant, and which of God's truths were indispensable.

Best of all, the people of heaven will include many of our family and friends. What a joy it will be to reunite with those who had been cut off by death! But how will we know them? Will they look young or old? Will they have the same blemishes and deformities by which we

19

formerly recognized them? And in the vast expanse of the heavenly city, how will we ever find them? I don't know the answer to all of these questions, but when I get to heaven I could solve most of the problem with two simple suggestions: (1) We all wear name tags, and (2) We publish a city directory. (And if I can think of a way to handle the problem, rest assured that God can do it better!)

We will certainly retain our individual personalities in heaven. Like the angels, saints in heaven still have their names (as did Moses and Elijah centuries after death), and they will still have their memories of who they were (as did the rich man and Lazarus). On judgment day people will know very well whether they had fed the hungry, clothed the naked, and visited the sick. We will all know exactly who we are, even if our glorified bodies are not immediately recognizable to others. We will know that there are people we want to see, as when David said of his deceased baby, "I will go to him, but he will not return to me" (2 Sam 12:23).

God does not deal with people in bulk quantity. Each person is responsible for his or her own sins. Each person who will inherit salvation is carefully listed — by name — in the Lamb's book of life. Therefore heaven will not be a vast sea into which our cup of life is poured. *We will not lose our individuality in heaven.* Our shepherd knows his sheep by name and calls us one by one into his eternal fold.

But one nagging question may linger: Will we be given the opportunity to rejoin our family and friends, or will we be required to focus all our attention on God? Is God a jealous God, resenting any love directed to anyone else? This issue is solved for us by God himself. He is the one who first commanded, "Love one another." He is

We will not lose our individuality in heaven.

the one who wants us to have fellowship with him and with one another (1 John 1:7). We should have complete confidence that God will allow — and encourage — all the special reunions of heaven. (More on this in Lesson Six.)

> Greater than the angels, greater than his people, God is the real reason for heaven.

So take a few minutes to contemplate all the people you want to see in heaven. Make a list — savor each entry. This will get you hungry for heaven! There are missionaries who were killed on foreign fields . . . there are schoolmates who died in their youth . . . there are moms and dads, aunts and uncles, grandparents. (My great-great-grandfather was a preacher. I'd sure like to get to know him.) Add to your list all the interesting people in history who will be in heaven. Then put down your favorite characters in the Bible. Imagine getting to spend an afternoon with David or Elijah or Ruth. Finally, make a list of all the people who will want to see you in heaven. Don't disappoint them!

GOD

We have saved the best for last. Central among the inhabitants of heaven will be God. *Greater than the angels, greater than his people, God is the real reason for heaven.* Of all the things we enjoy in heaven, the best will be the time we spend adoring our God. Let's consider meeting God in heaven, in the person of the Spirit, the Son, and the Father.

For as many years as we have been Christians, we have had a constant companion — the Holy Spirit. He dwells within us, strengthening our inner man. When we get to heaven the presence of the Spirit should seem like a familiar thing, since he is the Person of the Godhead we have already encountered. However, all of our experience with the Holy Spirit now is only a down payment, a mere foretaste of the richer fellowship in heaven. (See 2 Cor 1:22; 5:5; and Eph. 1:13-14. For further discussion on the role of the Holy Spirit in heaven, see Lesson Seven.)

Jesus the Son of God will be much more conspicuous in heaven. Revelation 1:13-18 depicts him as a powerful warrior, with fiery eyes and a sharp two-edged sword coming from his mouth. Many of the other passages in the Revelation depict him as the Lamb that was slain. At the same time, he will still be the same Jesus whom we came to know in the pages of the four Gospels. He will sit beside the Father on the throne of heaven. We will gather with all the other saints and proclaim that Jesus is "worthy . . . to receive power and wealth and wisdom and strength and honor and glory and praise" (Rev 5:12). At long last we will have the same privilege as his disciples in the first century. We will see him with our own eyes and hear his very words. We will no longer need to envy Thomas, who was invited to touch his pierced hands and side. We will no longer need to envy Mary, who was allowed to pour the perfume of her devotion on his head and feet, wiping them with her hair. One of the greatest joys of heaven will be meeting Jesus face to face!

God the Father is the centerpiece of heaven. He sits on the throne, surrounded by angelic creatures who cry, "Holy, holy, holy!" and by the elders who lay their crowns at his feet (Rev 4:2-11). It was for his pleasure and glory that the whole universe, including mankind, was created. People from every nation and tribe and language will shout that "blessing and glory and wisdom and thanksgiving and honor and power and might [belong] to our God forever and forever" (Rev 7:12, NASB).

Jesus the Son of God will be much more conspicuous in heaven.

22

Many Christians feel a secret uneasiness about standing before the presence of God. We are eager to see Jesus (because we feel like we know him), but God the Father seems distant and frightening. If this has bothered you as well, consider this. *The very things that we love the most in the best people we know are the parts of their character that reflect the image of God.* Try to picture the personality of God as a composite of all that is warm and decent and good in the people you love. Could you learn to love a God like that? Would you want him to come down into your heavenly city and live right in the midst of his people? Would you want him to be the One to wipe every tear from your eyes? Would you let him be your Father?

Going to heaven doesn't seem so scary to me anymore. I look forward to seeing the angels; I long to meet all the people. I want to have fellowship with all the saints. I want to be surrounded by the people I know and love, and by people I would love to get to know. Best of all I want to be close to God — the Father, the Son, the Spirit. It sure will be good to get to heaven.

> The very things that we love the most in the best people we know are the parts of their character that reflect the image of God.

REFLECTING ON LESSON TWO

1. What do you find intriguing about angels?

2. Why do some people have more interest in angels than in God?

3. What do you think about all those crowds of people in heaven? What is it about crowds that you don't like? Will that still be true in heaven?

4. Who are the top five people in history you would like to meet in heaven?

5. How do you expect to find your family in heaven?

6. Do you think you will be able to touch Jesus?

7. Does meeting God seem scary to you?

3
T H R E E

WILL WE HAVE REAL BODIES AND WALK ON REAL STREETS OF GOLD?

While 81% of Americans believe in heaven, only 26% believe we will have bodies when we get there. Most people believe we will exist only as souls (*TIME/CNN* poll, March 24, 1997). Where does this idea come from? What does the Bible say?

THE INFLUENCE OF GREEK PHILOSOPHY

Some of our ideas about heaven come more from the Greeks than from God. The philosopher Plato, for instance, taught that the human soul was a prisoner in a physical body. Since the soul is more pure and godlike, at death it will rise upward while the debased body sinks into the earth. Plato taught that the highest realm of existence is the realm of reason and mind, far removed from the crudities of physical life.

The philosophy that sees the body as evil and the mind as good is called Dualism. During the first two or three centuries after the church was founded, some Christians tried to combine this philosophy with the gospel. For them, salvation meant ultimate escape from their bodies by knowing secret truths. Because of their emphasis on "knowing," they were called Gnostics (from the Greek word *gnosis*, "knowledge"). They believed that Jesus did not have a real body, and left no footprints when he walked in the sand. They further believed that the final goal of life was to attain a pure spirit existence, just like Jesus. In the heaven of the Gnostics, physical bodies would be only an unhappy memory. Spirit is superior to matter on earth, and so would it be in heaven.

At the end of the fourth century the most important Christian writer was Augustine. In his early writings he espoused the dualistic philosophies of Neoplatonism and the Gnostics. Augustine supposed that in the original garden Adam existed only as a soul. When Adam sinned, the penalty of his fallen state was to be put in a physical body. Regaining paradise would mean that the descendants of Adam would once again exist only as souls. Augustine eventually got over this mistaken view of things, but much of the rest of the world has not. They cannot see how real bodies have any place in paradise.

THE BODY AS A CREATION OF GOD

If we are going to have the right view of things, it is extremely important that we get started in the right direction from the very beginning. *When God created the world, the crowning achievement was the human race.* He made Adam from the dust of the ground and breathed into him the breath of life. Adam became "a living soul," a combination of body, mind, soul, and spirit. When God had also made Eve as Adam's equivalent with the same kind of flesh, mind, etc., he surveyed his handiwork and pronounced it "good," even "very good." *Though Plato, Augustine, and*

When God created the world, the crowning achievement was the human race.

26

a host of others had called the physical body bad, God said it was good.

When Jesus came into this world, he "became flesh and made his dwelling among us." This is the central truth of the incarnation. It was not impossible or unthinkable for Jesus as divine Spirit to clothe himself in "carnal" flesh. In fact, John warned that those who deny that Jesus came in the flesh were deceivers and antichrists (2 John 7). If there were any question about the value of the physical body, Jesus settled the matter with his incarnation.

Though Plato, Augustine, and a host of others had called the physical body bad, God said it was good.

Likewise, when Jesus came forth from the tomb at his resurrection, he was still in his body. He was not pure spirit. He allowed women to hug his feet; he invited Thomas to examine his wounds; he ate bread and fish. "Touch me and see," he said to his disciples. "A ghost does not have flesh and bones, as you see I have" (Luke 24:39). If the body were inherently evil, Jesus should have shed it at the tomb!

THE GLORIFIED BODY

One of the central truths of Scripture, as witnessed in the historic creeds, is that our bodies will be raised. The same Lord who called Lazarus from the dead will one day command that the grave and sea give up their captives. "Do not be amazed at this," Jesus said, "for a time is coming when all who are in their graves will hear his voice and come out — those who have done good will rise to live, and those who have done evil will rise to be condemned" (John 5:28-29). When the Lord himself comes down from heaven, he will issue a loud command and the dead will rise (1 Thess 4:16).

Scripture is quite clear that we will have bodies. We were made both body and soul; we shall be redeemed and glorified in both body and soul. We will not "escape" our bodies and exist as spirits alone. "We know that if the earthly tent we live in is destroyed, we have a building from God, an eternal house in heaven, not built by human hands. . . . For while we are in this tent, we groan and are burdened, because we do not wish to be unclothed but to be clothed with our heavenly dwelling, so that what is mortal may be swallowed up by life" (2 Cor 5:1,4).

But Scripture is also quite clear that our bodies will be changed. In 1 Cor 15:35-49 Paul goes to great lengths to explain this grand concept. When a seed is planted in the ground, the plant it produces is much more than the seed from which it came. And just as there are different kinds of flesh — beef, poultry, fish — we should not be surprised that there is a difference in the earthly body and the heavenly body. The heavenly body will have a different degree of splendor (but it will still be a body). It will be purified, immortalized, and empowered (but it will still be a body). In lesson four we will explore some of the possibilities of the glorified body, but for now let us be content with this conclusion: there will be a body. Let us eagerly await the coming of the Lord Jesus, who will "transform our lowly bodies so that they will be like his glorious body" (Phil 3:21).

THE STREETS OF GOLD

Now let's return to the Bible's description of the garden of Eden for another clue into what we can reasonably expect to find in heaven. A river flowed from the land of Eden, with one of its branches flowing "around the entire land of Havilah, where gold is found" (Gen 2:11). Then comes a statement that is

Scripture is quite clear that we will have bodies.

28

most interesting. Whereas we have an inborn philosophy that gold is material and "bad," God's Word says, "The gold of that land is good."

Why is it so unthinkable that God would pave his city streets with pure gold?

We somehow know that streets of gold in heaven cannot be literally true, but on what do we base that conclusion? In the garden of Eden God made gold and all kinds of precious jewels, and thought it was a good thing. In heaven, according to John's revelation, the streets will be paved with gold and the city walls will be encrusted with giant jewels. (Cf. Rev 21:18-21.) The gold will be "pure gold, as pure as glass." The gold will not be transparent, of course, but its degree of purity will match that of transparent glass, which cannot hide any impurities. *Why is it so unthinkable that God would pave his city streets with pure gold?*

A RESTORED PARADISE

There are, in fact, a good number of similarities between the garden of Genesis and the paradise of Revelation. (Incidentally, our word "paradise" comes from an old Persian word meaning "garden.") Note the following comparisons, adapted from the book *Heaven* by Bob Chambers (College Press, 1991):

GENESIS	REVELATION
God made heaven and earth (1:1)	New heaven and earth (21:1)
God made light (1:3)	God gives light (22:5)
Two great lights (1:16)	The light of God and the Lamb (21:23)
It was very good (1:31)	There is nothing impure (21:27)
Tree of life (2:9)	Tree of life (22:2)
A river (2:10)	River of crystal clear water (22:1-2)

Gold in the land (2:11-12)	Pure gold (21:18,21)
Man put there to work (2:15)	Men will serve God (22:3)
God seeks fellowship (3:8)	God dwells with his people (21:3)

Because of the sin of Adam and Eve, the original paradise was lost. In the restored paradise the following contrasts may be noted:

GENESIS	REVELATION
The serpent deceived them (3:13)	The devil is cast into the lake of fire (20:10)
God increases pains (3:16)	No more pain (21:4)
Cursed is the ground (3:17)	No longer any curse (22:3)
To dust man must return (3:19)	No more death (21:4)
Kept from tree of life (3:24)	Have the right to the tree of life (22:13)

In many ways, then, *the story of salvation is the story of paradise lost and paradise restored.* Heaven will be more wonderful than the garden of Eden, of course, just as the glorified body is greater than the "seed" body planted in the grave. But what is wrong with thinking of heaven as a real place, with robust pleasures for real bodies?

A RENEWED CITY

In Revelation 21:2 heaven includes a beautiful city, the new Jerusalem. An angel uses a gold measuring rod to determine the size of the city. It is immense — 1400 miles wide and long and high! Now, if all this is merely figurative and the actual size is irrelevant, why should the angel go to all the bother of measuring? And if we already have great metropolitan areas stretching unbroken for 100 miles, why should 1400 miles seem incredible? Or is it only the

The story of salvation is the story of paradise lost and paradise restored.

height of the city that we cannot accept? Personally, I am becoming more and more open to the idea that God described heaven as it actually is!

The new Jerusalem is described as a place with a clear river, with a tree that bears a new crop of fruit every month, with plenty of space for all God's children. It has walls 200 feet thick, but the gates never need to be closed. We will be free from all danger, and we will have free access from the central city into the rest of heaven. Each gate is described as a giant pearl. Shall we believe God can make a pearl as big as a city gate?

> The best thing about living in the heavenly Jerusalem is that God will live there with us!

Even more important than the riches of the heavenly city will be its permanence. (What good would all the gold and jewels be if we knew we'd have to give them up?) In our lives on earth we can never be entirely sure that we will not lose our houses or be evicted from our apartments. But when Jesus promised that his Father's house had "many rooms" (or "mansions," KJV), his word in John 14:2 emphasizes the concept "remain" or "abide" or "stay." It is not the glory of heaven that is important to us; it is the permanence.

And yet there remains one thing in the renewed city that is even more important. *The best thing about living in the heavenly Jerusalem is that God will live there with us!* When John saw the Holy City he heard a loud voice saying, "Now the dwelling of God is with men, and he will live with them" (Rev 21:3). This was also the promise of Jesus: "I will come back and take you to be with me that you also may be where I am" (John 14:3). This is the best of all!

REFLECTING ON LESSON THREE

1. Where does the average person get his or her ideas about heaven?

2. What was the philosophy of Dualism? How did it affect the way some people thought about Jesus? How did it affect the way they thought about heaven?

3. Is the body a good thing or a bad thing? Is flesh inherently evil?

4. Why do we need bodies for heaven? Why not just leave them in the grave?

5. In what ways will heaven be a "restored paradise"?

6. Be honest. Do you personally think heaven will have streets made of gold?

7. What is the good and the bad about living in a city? How might this apply to the new Jerusalem in heaven?

4

F O U R

WILL OUR BODIES HAVE ALL FIVE SENSES?

Now it's time to speculate. While Scripture is quite clear that we shall have bodies in heaven, we do not know exactly what those bodies will be like. The best we can do is to make an educated guess based on certain clues in God's Word. We will need to exercise some humility here, and admit our limitations. But it is entirely proper to get excited about what God may have in store for us, because he has no limitations!

IN THE BEGINNING

Imagine you are Adam or Eve, and you have just come to life in the garden of Eden. Can you see the blue skies, white clouds, and green grass? Can you smell the flowers? Can you hear the birds? This paradise has a wonderful variety of things to behold. God has made it all, and he has put you there in a body so you can enjoy it. Each of the five senses in your brand new body has been designed by God. Surrounding you in the garden paradise are all the sights and sounds and smells which God has provided to bring you pleasure. He has pronounced it all "very good."

Now, of course you are not Adam or Eve, but you still live in a world that in many ways is an extension of Eden. The same plants and animals, colors and smells, sounds and flavors still exist. Your body has the same five senses as Adam and Eve had, so you continue to enjoy the pleasures God provides. Which of these five senses should be taken away to make our heavenly bodies better? To put it another way, *when we get to heaven shall we expect less — or more — than the pleasures of this present world?*

THE SENSE OF TASTE

My tongue can distinguish a wonderful variety of flavors. Every time I enjoy a meal I ought to thank God for my sense of taste. The human tongue can recognize — and enjoy — literally thousands of different kinds of foods and flavors. It is surprising, then, to learn that there are only four kinds of taste buds on the tongue. On the tip are the taste buds which respond to salty and sweet flavors. At the base are the taste buds for bitter; along the edges are the taste buds for sour. Every flavor we experience is merely a specific combination of these four taste buds working together. Do you suppose that when God invented four kinds of taste buds he could not think of any more?

There will most certainly be things to taste and food to eat in heaven. (Or did you think that food is so wicked, so material, that real saints will fast through all eternity?) John's revelation says those who overcome can eat the hidden manna, sit down at the marriage feast of the Lamb, and enjoy the new crop of fruit every month on the tree of life. Do you suppose there could be any new flavors there? Remember: heaven will

When we get to heaven shall we expect less — or more — than the pleasures of this present world?

34

be more — not less — than the life we presently enjoy.

THE SENSE OF SMELL

Smells have a wonderful way of bringing us pleasure. A certain aroma can instantly transport us across two decades and a thousand miles to Grandma's kitchen. A perfume can suddenly recall romance. All the different scents we smell are detected by just seven types of smell receptors inside our noses. Do you suppose God exhausted the possibilities when he invented these seven? What a variety of combinations is already possible!

The human nose can detect as little as one twenty-five thousandth of a milligram of musk oil in a litre of air. We think of our noses as pretty efficient. It is humbling to observe that God put a better nose on nearly all of the animal world. A lowly male silkworm can detect a female at a distance of two miles! *Even your dog smells better than you do.* Since, then, God has already demonstrated that he is capable of building a better nose, why should we not expect a superior sense of smell in heaven? And why should we not expect heaven to have a greater variety of things to smell than even the garden of Eden?

THE SENSE OF HEARING

I suffer from a nerve loss in my hearing. One of my favorite expectations about heaven is that I will be able to throw away my hearing aids! In the meantime I am frequently reminded that there are many, many sounds we just don't want to miss: a baby's cooing, a bird's chirp, a beautiful symphony, a gentle word of love. Even with acute hearing, however, we cannot hear much higher or lower than the range of a concert piano keyboard. (Imagine the possibilities of a heavenly harp! There really will be harps, you know.) Animals hear much more keenly than we do. *Your dog not only smells better than you do, he also hears better.* He can hear higher, lower, and softer sounds. A porpoise can hear as high as 150,000 hertz, while humans can hear only as high as 20,000 hertz. Human hearing is wonderful, but obviously limited.

God has already demonstrated he can design ears superior to what we now have. Can you imagine a kind of hearing that is not only fully restored — but also improved? Can you imagine new kinds of sounds to hear and enjoy? A passage of Scripture comes to mind. It originally referred to the church, but could surely also apply to heaven: "No eye has seen, no ear has heard, no mind has conceived what God has prepared for those who love him" (1 Cor 2:9).

THE SENSE OF TOUCH

Does your heaven allow for a sense of touch? Or did you think we would float around and pass right through each other like ghosts? Will there be the warmth of a hug — the coolness of a breeze? Will there be the smooth perfection of soft skin, as flawless as a baby's? Will we feel the pleasure of muscle tone? Is there any reason why we should not?

It is interesting to read in the Gospels how much Jesus touched. Little children, filthy lepers, tearful women — he stretched out his hand and touched them. The Son of God on earth used and approved of the sense of touch. Why should it be eliminated in heaven? A heaven full of robust pleasures, solid to the touch, is the heaven of Scripture. Is it also the heaven of your imagination?

> Your dog not only smells better than you do, he also hears better.

36

Another type of feeling might be briefly mentioned here. There is a sense in which we also "feel" with our emotions. Sometimes these feelings are even sharper and deeper than our sensory feelings. Will we feel things emotionally in heaven? Will there be excitement, love, contentment, adoration? How could there be anything less?

> The heavenly Inventor of the eyeball and the rainbow has probably not completely run out of new ideas!

THE SENSE OF SIGHT

Our most precious sense is surely our sense of sight. God invented the eye, with its cones and rods scattered across the retina. He invented the fovea, where the photoreceptors are densely clustered so that we can focus more sharply. The lens, the cornea, the optic nerve — they are all parts of his handiwork. With our eyes we detect light, color, intensity, movement, and distance. We may not have the eyes of a hawk, but we think we see things pretty well.

It was a bit surprising when scientists learned that we can see only a small section of the total wavelength of light waves. We call that small band "visible light." In the full spectrum of light the wavelengths go a billion times shorter than the human eye can see (such as ultraviolet and X-rays.) The wavelengths go ten billion times longer than the eye can see (such as infrared radiation). Even with 20/20 vision we are missing most of the show!

In heaven God himself will provide our light. Will we be able to see the full spectrum? Will we see colors we never imagined? Will there be an unending variety of things to see? *The heavenly Inventor of the eyeball and the rainbow has probably not completely run out of new ideas!*

An analogy may help us envision the possibilities of heaven. Some people are color-blind. There may be a riot of color all around them, but they see only dull shades of gray or brown. The reality is there, but they do not have the sensitivity to detect it. In a similar fashion I suppose all of us are presently "heaven blind." Like the servant of Elisha, we need to have someone pray, "O LORD, open his eyes so he may see" (2 Kings 6:17). The hills may be full of angels and chariots of fire, but we are too dull to see them. We are like people who are tone-deaf, color-blind, with taste and smell dulled by disease, with a callused sense of touch. And then we are foolish enough to suppose we have already experienced all of God's reality!

A SIXTH SENSE?

In regard to the senses of the human body, there is no reason to suppose that they must somehow be limited to the number five. God can not only increase the receptors of our present senses; he can create whole new senses for us. It could even be that we already have senses which we cannot presently use. For instance, a person with perfectly good vision would not even know he had it if he had always lived in the darkness. I have no idea what additional senses I might already have or might someday enjoy, but I am willing to leave that up to God.

The whole point of this excursus on the senses of the human body is to excite your imagination about your heavenly body. The joys of paradise need to become so real to you that you can almost taste them. *Your mouth needs to water as you grow hungry for heaven.* A bland, lifeless existence has no attraction, but heaven will be a place where you

Your mouth needs to water as you grow hungry for heaven.

can taste, smell, hear, touch, and see. We have often said heaven is "a prepared place for prepared people"; we should also teach that it is "a real place for real people!"

REFLECTING ON LESSON FOUR

1. Was there anything lowly or debased about the bodies of Adam and Eve? Did God design them to live in a fallen world?

2. How do we know our present senses could be improved?

3. Have you thought of heaven as being dull and bland? What is the typical view of heaven in the comic strips, in TV commercials, or in the movies?

4. If there is food in heaven for us to taste and smell and eat, will we have complete digestive tracts?

5. Why should there be a sense of touch in heaven?

6. What would it be like to live in heaven with any one of the five senses removed? What will it be like to live there with improved senses, or with whole new senses?

7. When you think of the possibilities of your heavenly body, what part do you find the most exciting?

5

F I V E

WHAT WILL NOT BE IN HEAVEN?

Massive unemployment! Millions of people thrown out of work! No, that's not the picture of a bear market on Wall Street; that's the picture of heaven. Just think of it. All those people who sell padlocks and burglar alarms won't be necessary in a place where thieves will not break through and steal. And the people who make Kleenex won't be needed, since God himself will wipe away every tear. There will be no more sickness (or doctors or nurses or hospitals). There will be no criminals (or policemen or judges . . . there'll be no lawyers in heaven!). There will be no more pain, no more death, no more need to insure ourselves against calamity.

In fact, the odds are strong that what you presently do for a living won't be necessary in heaven. But if you're starting to worry about how you'll earn a paycheck, there is no need for concern. In heaven the mortgage payments are a thing of the past, because Jesus has prepared for us a place in the Father's house. The food bills are taken care of, so we will not hunger or thirst anymore. The moths will not eat holes in our clothes, nor will any other destructive force be at work. The gates of the heavenly city will be unlocked, both day and night. Life in heaven is going to be very different from life on earth. (And if you are worried about what these unemployed people are going to do with all that time on their hands, we'll cover that in Lesson Six.) Right now in this lesson we will consider the implications of a few more things that are specifically said not to exist in heaven.

> One of the best things about heaven is that the devil won't be there.

NO MORE DEVIL (REV 20:10)

One of the best things about heaven is that the devil won't be there. This means we won't ever be bothered by temptation again, for the Tempter himself will be gone. Imagine the joy and freedom that will be ours when temptation is a thing of the past! We who hunger and thirst for righteousness will finally get what we want in heaven. We who, like Paul in Romans 7, have struggled against "the evil that we do not want to do" will have the final victory.

With the devil out of the picture there will be no more lying and deceiving. He was a liar from the beginning and is the father of lies (John 8:44). He lied to Adam and Eve; he has lied to you and me. But he won't be there to lie to us in heaven. With that old deceiver out of the way, we will be free to practice truth. White lies and all the shades of gray will be a thing of the past. Imagine living in a place where we can finally be completely open and honest with everyone. (This will take a little getting used to for most of us!)

When the devil has been cast down into hell, there will be nothing impure or unclean (Rev 21:27). Even the river of the great city will be crystal clear, free from any pollution. Right now, however, that's not true of any big

41

city on earth. We have to purify our water, choke on our smog, and put up with foreign chemicals in our food. Worse than that is the moral pollution that fills our airwaves and computer lines. But heaven will be sparkling clean.

While we're on the subject of the devil, let's not waste any sympathy over his final demise. He is not like a rival suitor competing for your affections; he is your enemy. (The very name Satan is a Hebrew word meaning "enemy" or "adversary.") *He is not trying to get you to come and live with him in hell; he is trying to destroy you.* (He is called "the Destroyer," and "a murderer from the beginning.") Just as with Job in the Old Testament, the devil is trying to drive a wedge between us and God by accusing us of disloyalty and sin. (The name "devil" is literally "accuser" in the Greek.) When he is cast into the lake of fire forever he will be getting exactly what he deserves.

NO MORE CURSE (REV 22:3)

Near the end of John's revelation is a simple statement so brief you might well overlook it. With no elaboration or explanation he says, "No longer will there be any curse." The curse of the fallen world (Gen 3:16-20) will finally be lifted. The day toward which all creation has groaned as if in the pains of childbirth (Rom 8:22) will finally come.

Consider what it has meant to live under the curse of a fallen world. We live in a world where there is a constant threat of pain. From our mother's pain in childbirth to our children's pain at our funeral, there is pain. From the bruises of childhood to the aching muscles of adult labor, there is pain. God warned Adam and Eve,

> Satan is not trying to get you to come and live with him in hell; he is trying to destroy you.

42

but they plunged themselves and all their descendants into a world of pain. If God could have kept the world the way he designed it, there would have been no pain.

In a fallen world under the curse, thorns infest the ground. Germs infest our bodies; insects infest our fields and homes. Toil that could

> God did not want us to have to live under a curse in a fallen world.

have been productive is often wasted. Worse yet, flawed chromosomes begin to infest our genetic pool. They are the result of radiation, toxic chemicals, unfiltered sunlight — they are the result of living in a fallen world. It is remarkable then that when babies are born with genetic birth defects we assume God wanted it that way. Such things happen in a fallen world, but they would never have happened if that first paradise could have stayed the way God made it. Sickness, disease, deformity, and death are not what God wanted for us. He gave very explicit warnings to Adam and Eve so these could be avoided. Someday, when the world is once again the way God wants it to be, there will no longer be any curse.

People who live in a fallen world live under the curse of death. It doesn't take most of us very long to notice that our bodies are wearing out. We keep our scars, but lose our hair. We accumulate the fat we don't want, but lose the muscle mass we need. Every time we see someone we haven't seen for twenty years, we cannot help but notice how the years are taking their toll. Sometimes the mind wears out before the body does. People who have known us all their lives will stare blankly at us without a flicker of recognition. When we watch our loved ones' bodies and minds fail, we are tempted to grow bitter against God. Why does he want to do this to us? In fact, he doesn't. *He did not want us to have to live under a curse in a fallen world.* When he made the world the way he wanted it to be and pronounced it "very good," there was no curse. And when the new heaven and earth are once again the way he wants them to be, there will no longer be any curse.

Living under a curse in a fallen world means that we sometimes suffer tragic consequences. A drunken driver may kill our children; an armed robber may kill a friend. Worn brakes may fail; tired eyes may fall asleep; tires may lose their traction. Accidents happen. When they do, it is not because God delights in such things. In fact, if he had had his way in the beginning, none of these things would ever happen. They are part of the curse of the fallen world. God's heaven will have no curse — and that tells us a very great deal about what God is really like.

NO MORE TEMPLE (REV 21:22)

It is most remarkable that the new Jerusalem in John's revelation has no temple. What is the holy city without its temple? No sooner had David made his city on the hill of Zion than he started planning for the house of God. His son Solomon built the first temple, which stood for 400 years. After the fall of Jerusalem and the time of rebuilding, the second temple stood for almost 500 years. The final, lavish temple constructed by Herod the Great was one of the most beautiful buildings on earth. *But there will be no temple in heaven. Why?*

One reason the temple will no longer be needed is its primary role in animal sacrifice. The priests of the old covenant didn't spend much time studying and teaching God's Word; they were too busy butchering and burning animals. In the new covenant our high priest Jesus Christ has offered himself as

But there will be no temple in heaven. Why?

44

the final sacrifice. He has atoned for our sins once and for all. *Heaven will need no more sacrifices; hence, no more temple.*

Perhaps there is a more significant reason for the absence of the temple. The original temple had an elaborate system of divisions to designate how close people could get to God. God's glory was present in the inner sanctuary, the Holy of Holies. Only the high priest could enter that room, and he could do so only once a year. The outer room, the Holy Place, was accessible only to the priests. They entered this room to tend the lamp, to put fresh bread on the table, and to keep the altar of incense burning. Outside the temple the men of Israel could stand in their courtyard to be near the altar where animal sacrifices were made. Outside this area was the courtyard of the women. They could come this close and put their donations in the treasury receptacles, but no closer. Even further outside was the courtyard of the Gentiles. They were strictly forbidden to come any closer. (Archaeologists in Jerusalem have unearthed first century signs which read: "No Gentile may enter inside the enclosing screen around the Temple. Whoever is caught has himself to blame for the death which follows.")

In the heavenly city there will no longer be a place where people are separated into categories and told to stand back from God. Earlier in the same chapter of Revelation which notes the absence of the temple, John records the words of a loud voice from the throne: "Now the dwelling of God is with men, and he will live with them. They will be his people, and God himself will be with them and be their God. He will wipe every tear from their eyes" (Rev 21:3-4). No longer will God be remote and removed from his people. He will live in our midst, tenderly meeting our needs. With God immediately present, who needs a temple?

NO MORE SEA, NO MORE TIME

As a footnote to the bigger issues of this lesson, there remain two curious statements to be considered. The first is the comment in Rev 21:1 that when John saw the new heaven and new earth, "there was no longer any sea." For those of us who love to watch the waves crash against a rocky shore, this is a disappointment. The significance of this must be seen from a biblical perspective. Ancient people feared the ocean. It was a great barrier between lands, and often swallowed up those who tried to cross it. The wild, restless ocean was often portrayed as an enemy, whom only God could tame. The ocean's danger and separation will no longer trouble God's people in heaven.

The second curious passage to be considered is the translation of Rev 10:6 in the King James Version, which reads, ". . . there should be time no longer." This has often been misunderstood as meaning that time itself will no longer exist in heaven. While God's sense of time is certainly different from our own (2 Pet 3:8), *there is no reason to think we will have no sense of time in heaven.* We will certainly have an awareness of the sequence of events (I did this before I did that, etc.), so in at least some sense we will still have time. What the passage really means is that in the unfolding events of God's judgment on the earth, "There will be no more delay" (NIV). It is the equivalent of the timekeeper saying, "Time's up!"

> **There is no reason to think we will have no sense of time in heaven.**

When the trumpet of the Lord shall sound, and there will be no more time to get ready for judgment, God's people will have nothing to fear. They will be ushered into a land where there will be no crying, pain, or death. The devil will be cast out, the curse will be lifted, and God himself will dwell in the midst of his people. Part of what will make heaven so good is what *won't* be there.

REFLECTING ON LESSON FIVE

1. Will your occupation be needed in heaven? What occupations will be needed?

2. Have you ever thought of the devil as someone who is competing for your affections? What is he really trying to do?

3. Is lying ever acceptable? Will it be acceptable in heaven?

4. How has living under the curse in a fallen world affected you personally?

5. Why do we want to give God "credit" for causing all the tragedies of life?

6. Can you imagine approaching God without any restrictions or limitations?

7. Someday the cry will go out, "Time's up!" Will it come as a relief to you or as a warning of doom?

6
S I X

WHAT WILL WE DO WITH ALL THAT TIME?

Have you ever been in a song service that went a bit too long? In fact, you thought it would never end? What if heaven is just one big, long song service? Huckleberry Finn thought "all a body would have to do was to go around all day long with a harp and sing, forever and ever." Mark Twain said he thought a vacation in Bermuda would be more interesting!

Augustine thought heaven would be like a monastery, an eternal continuation of the ascetic life. He said, "There we shall rest and see, see and love, love and praise. This is what shall be in the end without end." The only activity of heaven will be "to stand, to see, to love, to praise." At the risk of sounding unspiritual, most of us would privately admit that this kind of heaven doesn't sound all that attractive. One of my students once wrote, "I love God, and I love to sing his praises. But eternity seems like it could get a bit long."

To solve this dilemma, let's return to the beginning.

IN THE IMAGE OF GOD

Genesis 1:27 says, "So God created man in his own image, in the image of God he created him; male and female he created them." Alone of all creation, human beings are made in the image of God. But what is it about us that is "in the image of God"? And what are the implications of being made like this?

God is creative, intelligent, socially interactive, and loving. Humans are also like this.

There are several ways in which we are like God, but animals are not. These features could be at least part of "the image of God." For instance, *God is creative, intelligent, socially interactive, and loving. Far more than anything in the animal world, humans are also like this.* God made us this way . . . for heaven.

IN HIS IMAGE — CREATIVE

It is God's nature to create. He is the original Creator and all the universe is his creation. But humans he created to be like himself. Thus, we are inherently creative and inventive. We are dreamers and builders, always looking for new ways to do things. Variety is the spice of life, we say, and set out to design houses and cars and electronic gear that are better than anything previous. Given enough money, each of us could design and build our perfect dream house — and no two houses would be exactly alike.

By contrast, animals operate by instinct and do predictable things. A barn swallow will build a barn swallow nest — every time. A beaver, a wasp, a termite, an eagle — all will build the same kind of house that others of their species always build. They have no creativity; they have instinct. And they are perfectly happy, I suppose, doing the things they were created to do. Birds have wings, so they fly. Fish have fins, so they swim. The way they are designed fits the purpose God had in mind for them.

But *people are designed to create. God made us this way.* Why, then, should we think that God would make us creative, but put us in the kind of heaven where all we do is sing? I think the reason we resist the idea of an eternity-long song service is that it stifles our inner drive to be what God meant us to be. (Why give a bird wings if you never mean for it to fly?) Moreover, we were not designed "in the image of God" in order to live in a fallen world. We were designed this way to live in paradise.

Heaven will be a place where people exercise their creativity for the glory of God. Poets will write; musicians will compose; artists will paint. Builders and artisans will make an ever improving array of structures. In a thousand different ways we will be free to use our creativity to honor our Creator. "Be all you can be" will be the motto of heaven.

IN HIS IMAGE — INTELLIGENT

God is intelligent, even omniscient. More than any of the animals, humans rise toward this aspect of God's nature. This is not to say animals have no brain or that you can't teach an old dog new tricks. But at its best animal intelligence is primitive and instinctive. Only humans write encyclopedias, solve equations, learn to tear down an engine, or analyze life. We glorify God when we develop the intelligence he made possible, and when we use it for the good of his creation.

People are designed to create. God made us this way.

A mind is a terrible thing to waste. What a joy it will be in heaven when we finally have the time to

50

read, to learn, to expand our vision. What a pleasure it will be to learn from the great minds of the ages, and from God himself. We will never catch up with God, of course, but we will always be growing more like him. Perhaps we will understand the unified field theory

> In heaven our renewed bodies will have renewed minds, and learning will be a joy.

in heaven, something Stephen Hawking said would be "to know the mind of God." Perhaps we will have opportunity to learn about people who lived in distant lands, or in distant times. Perhaps we will finally have time to spend on all those pursuits we never had time for on earth.

Here's another exciting thought about intelligence in heaven. Learning can be fun again when our memories and our patience are not flawed. Little children love to learn. Their minds are fresh and eager. Older children begin to resist, until finally as adults we find it genuinely difficult to master new fields. Like a worn-out chalkboard, our minds just won't hold a clear image very well. But *in heaven our renewed bodies will have renewed minds, and learning will be a joy.*

IN HIS IMAGE — SOCIAL

From the beginning God has existed in a society, as Father and Son and Holy Spirit. It was completely within his nature to expand that perfect fellowship to include the angels of heaven and the people of earth. Like our Creator — but unlike mere animals — humans are socially interactive. It's true, of course, that birds of a feather flock together and sheep huddle together as a flock, but that is not fellowship. Animals have ways of primitive communication, but only people reach a level of fellowship that mirrors the social nature of God.

51

How shall we express this aspect of God's image in heaven? We could spend half an eternity just catching up with family and friends. Then there are all those people we wish we could have known better, but just never had the time. We could meet the saints, interview Moses, spend time with Robert E. Lee. *We could communicate without fear of misunderstanding, hidden motives, or selfish prejudice.* God's family could really have a great family reunion!

IN HIS IMAGE — LOVING

God is love. As much as any other word in the Bible, love expresses the central core of the nature of God. In ways that transcend the animal world, humans alone have been created with a capacity and a desire for love. A dog may wag his tail and lick your face, but this is not really the kind of love that reflects the image of God.

In heaven we shall finally be able to love with an intensity, an inclusiveness, and a purity that has not been possible here on earth. For one thing, most of our attempts to love each other are distorted by our sexuality. If I go to church and hug the ladies, I'd better be careful. I must not hug too tightly or too long. Like a magnet, I may feel the pull of sexual attraction and this may corrupt my love. If I go to church and hug the fellows, I still have to be careful. If I hug too tightly or too long, the magnet is reversed and both of us start wanting to push away. One sex attracts me too much, the other pushes me away. How then shall I love?

Jesus said that at the final resurrection "people will neither marry nor be given in marriage; they will be like the angels in heaven" (Matt 22:30). I understand this to mean

> **We could communicate without fear of misunderstanding, hidden motives, or selfish prejudice.**

52

that sexual attraction, once necessary to propagate the human race, will be eliminated. This does not mean I will not see and love my wife in heaven; it means that the circle of my love will be enlarged. I will love her no less; I will love the

> **Pure love can always be shared.**

rest of mankind as much. Most of us have already experienced this in part. When I married, the circle of my love included only my wife. In a few years the circle enlarged to include a daughter, and then a son. The love I felt for the child in my arms had nothing to do with sexual attraction; it was simply love. This year the circle increased again — a grandchild! As each new person enlarges my family circle, my love for others is not diluted or diminished. *Pure love can always be shared.* Consider what this can mean for enlarging the family circles of heaven until all our circles include each other. At last we will be able to love in total purity, intensity, and inclusiveness.

But, someone will surely object, should we not direct all our love toward God? Doesn't he demand that we love him, and him alone? Will he not require every eye and every thought to be on him? Scripture says no. The two greatest commandments of God's own Word are to love God and to love each other. It is by loving each other that we demonstrate that we are really his children, disciples of his Son. In fact, we cannot claim to love God if we do not love the very people who bear his image.

When the circle of my family grew to include a daughter and a son, my wife and I were concerned that they should learn to get along. They grew to love each other, and even now as adults they are the best of friends. Should my wife and I somehow feel threatened because our children love each other? Why, we have been delighted to see their love! In similar fashion, our wise heavenly Father is not jealous of the love his children show to each other. In fact, he commands it.

SPENDING OUR TIME — IN HIS IMAGE

What a wealth of things we will have to do and to be in heaven! Eternity hardly seems long enough for us to learn to live in God's image. *We will be free to express creativity, to learn endlessly, to socialize broadly, and to love intensely.* We will be surrounded by a host of other people who will be thrilled with their freedom to do the same. At the center of it all will be God, the pattern for our progress. Each part of our growth in his image will be to his glory and to his eternal pleasure.

Were heaven to be nothing more than a song service, much of what God made us to be would be wasted. It is no wonder that we inwardly resist any notion of such an eternal cage that would not let us flex our wings. That would not only forbid us to be what we want to be; it would prevent us from becoming and doing the very things for which God designed us. Thus, the description of the saints in John's revelation does not say, "They will sing forever"; it says, "And they will reign for ever and ever" (Rev 22:5).

We will be free to express creativity, to learn endlessly, to socialize broadly, and to love intensely.

54

REFLECTING ON LESSON SIX

1. At the gates of eternity will we be told, "Either join the choir or go to hell"?

2. What does it mean to be created "in the image of God"? What are other parts of God's image not mentioned in this lesson, but also designed into the human race?

3. How do people feel when their creativity is squelched?

4. If you only had the time, what would you really like to learn? Would this be allowed in heaven?

5. What if you don't like crowds and don't like having to meet new people? Try to analyze what makes you feel that way now, and what might be different in heaven.

6. What do you think about the notion of love expanding the family circles in heaven?

7. You can often tell what a man plans to do with a vehicle by the way he equips it. Does this hold true with God and the way he has designed and equipped us?

7

WILL GOD STILL BE INVISIBLE?

What will God be like in heaven? Will we be able to see him, hear him, *touch* him? Will he be more accessible there? How we answer these questions will have a lot to do with how eager we are to go to heaven.

Some may object that the whole idea of meeting God is totally unthinkable. God is simply too immense, too infinite, too transcendent. How could we even think about encountering the Mind who planned every cycle of nature, the Power who created the vastness of the universe, the Being who is everywhere present? And yet, God has made it clear from the beginning that he chooses to communicate — even fellowship — with the human race. In this lesson, then, we will grapple with a concept almost beyond comprehension: the ultimate nature of God, and how he has expressed himself to us in the form of the Father, the Son, and the Spirit.

THE GOD WHO CANNOT BE SEEN

No man has ever seen God, according to the opening verses of John's Gospel. This takes our minds back to

Adam, Noah, and Abraham. They all talked with God, but Scripture does not say they ever saw him. Then there was Moses, who was covered over as he hid in the cleft of a rock and was allowed to see only the trailing remnants of God's glory as he passed by on Mt. Sinai. Even Isaiah, when he saw a vision of the Lord, seems to have shifted his gaze immediately to the six-winged seraphs and away from God. *Throughout the Old Testament the God of Israel did not allow himself to be seen.*

> **Throughout the Old Testament the God of Israel did not allow himself to be seen.**

Certain passages in the New Testament seem to carry this a step further. God the Father not only must not be seen; he *cannot* be seen. He is "the King eternal, immortal, invisible" (1 Tim 1:17); the "invisible" One whom Moses could see only by faith (Heb 11:27); the "invisible God" (Col 1:15) who has "invisible attributes" (Rom 1:20, NASB). He is the One "whom no one has seen or can see" (1 Tim 6:16). "God is spirit," Jesus said, and that appears to seal the fact that God our Father is something like an invisible ghost.

FOR THEY SHALL SEE GOD

But two things must be considered before we rush to the conclusion that God is invisible and we will never be able to see him. The first is the range of meaning of the word "invisible." The Greek word used in all the New Testament passages can mean either "not seeable" or "not seen." In other words, it can mean either that God *cannot* be seen because his eternal nature is invisible, or that he *is not* seen because of our own inability to see him. Interestingly, the noun form of this word "invisible" occurs four times in the Old Testament and is always translated "blindness." In those passages the "not-seeing-ness" is in the eyes of the beholder, not in the permanent invisibility of the unseen object.

The second thing to be considered is even more important. *The New Testament says plainly that we will see God.* "Blessed are the pure in heart," Jesus said, "for they will see God" (Matt 5:8). A passage in Hebrews warns that "without holiness no one will see the Lord" (12:14), with the clear implication that if we do have holiness we will see him. Best of all is the description of heaven in the final chapter of Revelation: "The throne of God and of the Lamb will be in the city, and his servants will serve him. They will see his face" (22:3-4).

In the new Jerusalem, the dwelling of God will be with his people "and he will live with them" (Rev 21:3). We will see his face, hear his voice, and be in his immediate presence. No longer will our hearts plead, along with Philip, "Lord, show us the Father and that will be enough for us" (John 14:8). He whom we had previously seen only through the eyes of faith will be seen for real.

"SIR, WE WOULD LIKE TO SEE JESUS"

Along with the Greeks who came to the Passover in John 12, we "would like to see Jesus." Along with Mary Magdalene and Thomas in John 20 we would also like to touch him. Along with the disciples beside the sea or on a mountainside we would like to hear his words from his own lips. Will this ever be possible?

When Jesus was preparing his disciples for his departure, he made an important promise to them. He said he would prepare a place for them in the Father's dwellings, and one day he would return for them. "I will come back," he said, "and take you to be with me" (John 14:2-3). He certainly did not insinuate that their future reunion would

The New Testament says plainly that we will see God.

58

be something of a diminished fellowship. *Those original apostles, later including Paul, lived with an eager expectation of going to live with Jesus.* Peter assured his readers they would receive "a rich welcome into the eternal kingdom of our Lord and Savior Jesus Christ" (2 Pet 1:11). Paul spoke of his eager desire "to depart and be with Christ, which is better by far" (Phil 1:23).

> Those original apostles lived with an eager expectation of going to live with Jesus.

Likewise, the Lord Jesus is vividly pictured in the holy city of John's revelation. He is a majestic Ruler, yet a gentle Shepherd. He is the Lion of Judah, yet a slain Lamb. He is Lord of lords and King of kings, sharing the throne with the Father. He will judge the world, yet forgive those whose names are in his Book of Life. He is the conquering Christ, the Lamp of heaven, the divine Groom who awaits the wedding feast with his bride, the church. In every one of these roles he interacts with the human race, providing for our salvation and reaching out for our fellowship.

Jesus will not be like the person who becomes rich and famous, but forgets the friendship of the common folks he used to know. The Jesus we meet in heaven will be the same Jesus we knew in the Gospels. This should not surprise us, for Scripture assures us that he is "the same yesterday and today and forever" (Heb 13:8). He will still have the compassion that made him reach out to the outcasts, feed the hungry, and teach the lost. He will still have the gentle kindness that made him heal the crippled, forgive the fallen, and explain heavenly truths to dull earthly minds. He will still love people as they have never been loved before.

As we contemplate how wonderful it will be to live in the very presence of Jesus, we should remember that all his winsome traits are also the traits of the Father.

Though we have never seen the Father, Jesus has explained him to us (John 1:18). He was so much the embodiment of the invisible God that he could say, "Anyone who has seen me has seen the Father." All the things we love about Jesus, we will also love about the Father, for he and the Father are one (John 10:30).

AND WHAT OF THE HOLY SPIRIT?

God has also revealed himself to us in the Person of the Holy Spirit. The Spirit was present from the beginning of creation, "hovering" (as an eagle over her young) over the waters. Through the Old Testament the Spirit guided kings, inspired prophets, and empowered men like Samson. The promise was even made that one day God would pour out his Spirit on all people (Joel 2:28). In the New Testament Jesus promised that when he departed he would not leave his disciples as orphans, but would send "another Comforter." "If anyone loves me," Jesus went on to say, "he will obey my teaching. My Father will love him, and we will come to him and make our home with him" (John 14:23).

The promised Holy Spirit was given to all who repented and were baptized at Pentecost (Acts 2:38). The Spirit becomes a mark or seal of identification on every child of God, and anyone who does not have the Spirit does not belong to Christ (Rom 8:9). The Spirit is called a deposit or down payment (like "earnest money"), until we receive our final inheritance.

But what of the Holy Spirit in heaven? Curiously, the scenes of John's revelation almost never include the Holy Spirit. (The Spirit speaks messages to first century churches in chapters two and three, and utters a single sentence in 14:13. John is "carried . . . away in the Spirit" in 17:3 and 21:10,

> God has also revealed himself to us in the Person of the Holy Spirit.

60

and the Spirit issues a closing invitation in 22:17.) When the Father and the Lamb sit on the throne, the Spirit is never mentioned. This has led some to conclude that the Spirit, who was a temporary down payment to people on earth, will no longer be needed in heaven. The Spirit acted as an extension of God's presence on earth, but would not be necessary when God himself is immediately present in heaven.

> The manner of his indwelling in us may be temporary, but the Spirit himself is not temporary.

However, the Holy Spirit cannot be seen as only temporary. *The manner of his indwelling in us may be temporary, but the Spirit himself is not temporary.* Not only has the Spirit been around since the very beginning (Gen 1:2), Scripture further teaches us that he is "eternal" (Heb 9:14). Just like God the Father, the eternal Spirit is without beginning or end. His role in heaven will no doubt take on new dimensions, as he is visibly and personally present. We can be assured that he will be there.

EPILOGUE

The whole idea of meeting God — especially on judgment day — is understandably frightening. But repeatedly Scripture gives us reason to approach that day with confidence. Because of what Christ has done for us at the cross, we can "approach the throne of grace with confidence, so that we may receive mercy and find grace to help us in our time of need" (Heb 4:16). God is love, and we who live in God's love "will have confidence on the day of judgment" (1 John 4:17). On that day God's children can expect to hear this welcome: "Well done . . . . Come and share your master's happiness!" (Matt 25:21). Does this sound so bad?

REFLECTING ON LESSON SEVEN

1. What is the difference between "unseen" and "unseeable"?

2. Is God a spirit? Is he only a spirit? Since man is body-soul-spirit, could God be spirit and something more, as well?

3. Why is it easier to think about meeting Jesus in heaven than to think about meeting God?

4. What part of Jesus' personality do you find the most attractive?

5. How will Jesus be able to spend individual time with each one of the millions of people in heaven?

6. What do you think will be the role of the Holy Spirit in heaven? Will he still indwell us? Will he be visible to us in heaven?

7. Are you secretly afraid of standing before God on judgment day? What could you do to change this?

8

EIGHT

WHEN DOES IT ALL BEGIN?

OK, I'm sold on heaven. Where do I sign up? When can we leave? How soon can I expect to move into the new Jerusalem, greet the Lord, and start soaking up the sunshine of eternal bliss? Or is there some fine print on the bottom line?

DEATH: THE FINAL ENEMY

The harsh reality is that we have to die to go to heaven. True, there will be one generation who will get to see the Lord return, and that generation will get to skip the dying part. But the rest of us must leave this life through the doorway of death. As much as we try to put a good face on the situation, no one wants to die.

When we narrowly escape a head-on collision on a narrow highway, we breathe a big sigh of relief and thank the Lord for protecting us. When the doctor tells us we may have a fatal disease, we alert the church prayer-chain to plead for our healing. We try to avoid gangs, ghettos, and drive-by shootings. We exercise, take vitamins, and avoid fatty foods. We do everything in our power to delay our trip to heaven. What's the deal?

Actually, it is entirely normal and right that we should want to avoid death. *Scripture calls death our enemy, not our friend* (1 Cor 15:26). Death was not what God wanted in the first paradise, and he warned Adam and Eve not to do the thing that would make them die. Death became an ugly intrusion into the fallen world. People fell prey to disease, dangers, and death. Death represented the ultimate undoing of what God created. This is why Jesus did not rejoice at the tomb of Lazarus; instead, he wept.

So we have an unavoidable dilemma: we don't want to die, but we do want to go to heaven. Death is bad, but beyond death God will rescue us. Death is our enemy, but Jesus is our friend. We do not need to pretend that we look forward to the process of dying. We just need to rejoice that the God of life will defeat death for us and take us into his eternal home.

THE MOMENT OF DEATH

When we die, we are not alone. God will send his angels to escort us into his presence, just as he did for the beggar Lazarus. We do not need to fear the "unknown" or think that we will suddenly have no idea what we are supposed to do. We will join the great host of witnesses who have been cheering us on (Heb 12:1); we will have Jesus at our side to intercede for us; we will celebrate the fact that God is for us, not against us.

Some people see all this happening after a long delay, as the saints of the ages rise from their centuries of sleep. Others suppose that eternity is timeless, and in God's eyes all men die simultaneously and come to judgment day together. Still others believe that departed saints are already enjoying the presence of God while the rest of us are still living out our

Scripture calls death our enemy, not our friend.

64

lives here on earth. Which view is right?

IS THE REWARD "PUT ON LAYAWAY"?

Two passages of Scripture have led many people to believe that when we die we go into a state of suspended animation, sometimes called "soul-sleeping." Paul told the Corinthians that "the trumpet will sound, the dead will be raised imperishable, and we will be changed" (1 Cor 15:52). In greater detail Paul outlined for the people in Thessalonica how the Lord will come down with a loud command, with an archangel's call, and a trumpet blast. The dead in Christ who have "fallen asleep" will rise first, then those who are still alive will be caught up (the word is "raptured" in the Latin translation) to meet the Lord in the air. (See 1 Thess 4:13-18.)

As we shall see later in this lesson, however, there are many other Scriptures that speak of the departed saints going immediately into the presence of God. These other texts will deny that our reward is put on a layaway plan. Unless the Scriptures are to be left in contradiction to each other, it is best to understand these first two passages as referring to the resurrection of the body. *On the last day the graves and the sea will give up the captive, decayed bodies of saints who have long since been enjoying paradise.*

IS THE REWARD OUTSIDE OF TIME?

Perhaps the problem of a deferred reward versus an immediate reward can be solved another way. Both science and Scripture agree that time is not always the same.

Einstein proposed that time is relative, slowing down as one approaches the speed of light. Recent tests by NASA appear to confirm his idea. Peter assured his impatient readers that "with the Lord a day is like a thousand years, and a thousand years are like a day" (2 Pet 3:8). We even sing in an old hymn, "When the trumpet of the Lord shall sound and time shall be no more."

It is possible to see God as existing above and apart from our human time line. From his perspective in eternity *perhaps God can look down on the whole scope of human history at the same time.* While we experience the deaths of our loved ones as separated by a period of years, God could experience their deaths and welcome them all to heaven simultaneously. In this view, then, what we perceive as waiting in the grave for judgment day is simply our misunderstanding of time.

However, this view does not fit all the biblical data. The idea that there is no time at all in heaven, as noted in Lesson Five, is a mistranslation of Revelation 10:6. It is not that there will be no more time; rather, that there will be no more delay. Moreover, God's ability to wait for thousands of years before executing judgment does not say that those years do not exist. Those years simply underscore the long-suffering patience of God. But perhaps most fatal to the view of timelessness is the picture in Revelation 6:9-10. There the martyrs gather around God's throne to ask how long (note the time factor) before God avenges their deaths on those who are on the earth. In other words, while some are still living on earth, others have already died and gone to heaven. *All deaths are not simultaneous, after all.*

> Perhaps God can look down on the whole scope of human history at the same time.

IS THE REWARD IMMEDIATE?

A clear preponderance of Scriptures assures us that immediately upon

66

death we go to be with our Lord. We may want to call it "paradise" on this side of judgment day, and call it "heaven" after judgment day, but as long as we are in the presence of God there is probably little differ-

ence. The important thing is that we can have assurance about what happens when our loved ones die, and similarly, when we ourselves die. Included in the Scriptures that promise immediate reward are the following:

1. In the account of Lazarus and the rich man (which the Bible does not label as a parable), with Lazarus already carried by angels to Abraham's side and the rich man already in the fire, five brothers are still living back on earth (Luke 16:23).

2. To the penitent criminal on the cross Jesus said, "I tell you the truth, today you will be with me in paradise" (Luke 23:43).

3. When Martha spoke of "the resurrection at the last day," Jesus said in apparent correction of her statement, "Whoever lives and believes in me will never die" (John 11:26).

4. When Stephen was being stoned to death he saw Jesus standing at God's right hand in heaven, and he cried out, "Lord Jesus, receive my spirit" (Acts 7:55-59).

5. Paul said that as long as we live in our earthly bodies we are away from the Lord, and so he "would prefer to be away from the body and at home with the Lord" (2 Cor 5:6-8).

6. Facing possible execution at the hand of the Roman emperor, Paul said, "I desire to depart and be with Christ, which is better by far" (Phil 1:23).

7. With apparently no interval of soul-sleeping, "man is destined to die once, and after that to face judgment" (Heb 9:27).

8. Faithful Christians are surrounded by a cloud of witnesses, those who have already run the race. As they approach their final victory they come "to the city of the living God, the heavenly Jerusalem, and to innumerable angels in festal gathering, and to the assembly of the firstborn who are enrolled in heaven, and to God the judge of all, and to the spirits of the righteous made perfect, and to Jesus" (Heb 12:1,22-24, NRSV).

9. At the throne of God the martyrs cried out, "How long, Sovereign Lord, holy and true, until you judge the inhabitants of the earth and avenge our blood?" (Rev 6:10; cf. 20:4).

10. Every time deceased saints are pictured in Revelation they are awake and rejoicing in the presence of God (See Rev 7:9-17; 14:1-5; 15:2-8).

Scriptures clearly portray an immediate reward after we die. We can have assurance that *the old enemy death is defeated and turned into a doorway to eternal life.* Nothing — not even death itself — can separate us from the love of God that is in Christ Jesus our Lord (Rom 8:38). At the second coming of Jesus there may well be a single judgment day in which eternal destinies are publicly announced, but for those who have already gone to God's presence and for those who have just been snatched up from faithful life on earth, there is nothing to fear.

EPILOGUE

The old enemy death is defeated and turned into a doorway to eternal life.

In our efforts to imagine the grandeur of heaven and how God will take us there immediately upon death, we have no doubt fallen short of the mark. How can we know what it will really be like until we get there? But since we are so far inferior to our mighty God, we have surely exercised too little — not too much — imagination. Good heaven! What a wonderful place it must be!

REFLECTING ON LESSON EIGHT

1. Is it true that no one wants to die? How did Jesus feel about dying? What about Paul in the shipwreck? What would you say to a person who is deliberately trying to ruin his health so that he will die young?

2. Is it wrong to try to turn a funeral into a celebration?

3. In what sense do the dead "sleep" until Jesus returns?

4. Can you conceive of God looking down on the whole scope of human history simultaneously? Will there be any sequence of events, any "before" and "after" in heaven?

5. Which Scripture gives you the greatest personal assurance of what will happen to you when you die?

6. If life in God's presence is called "paradise" before judgment day, and "heaven" afterwards, what are the possible differences?

7. Did you wake up this morning thinking about heaven?

Kenny Boles is in his 29th year teaching Greek and New Testament at Ozark Christian College in Joplin, Missouri. He has written four other books for College Press, including the volume on Galatians and Ephesians in the NIV Commentary Series.

Kenny is a graduate of Ozark Christian College and Abilene Christian University (M.A. in Biblical and Patristic Greek). He has held located ministries in Tyro, KS, and Abilene, TX.

Kenny's wife, Linda, is also a graduate of Ozark Christian College. She teaches in the theatre department of Crowder College. Kenny and Linda have two children: Leigh Ann Johnson, whose husband Jeff is a youth minister in Kansas City; and Eric Boles, a graduate of OCC and Yale Divinity School. Their first grandchild, Sydney Grace Johnson, was born in July, 1998.